About the Book

Rufa *(Formica rufa)*, born into a wood ant colony, passes through many stages before becoming an adult worker. Taught by an older ant, Rufa becomes a forager, following the many trails from the anthill to gather pine needles which she piles up to protect the hill from rain, to fill her crop with sap from broken branches to feed other ants, and to perform the strange act of "milking" aphids of their nectar. On her return to the ant colony one day, Rufa barely manages to hide from an invading army of red ants, intent on stealing the wood ant eggs and using the hatchlings as red ant slaves. Rufa later becomes instrumental in restoring order in the devastated ant city and preparing for the winter hibernation.

Alice Hopf, whose *Biography of a Rhino* won the National Science Teacher's Award as one of the best science books of 1972, has here given us an equally exciting and informative account of a part of the ant world. More intriguing than fiction, her story is given special dimension by the precise, outstanding illustrations by naturalist artist Jean Zallinger.

Biography of an
Ant

BY ALICE HOPF

ILLUSTRATED BY JEAN ZALLINGER

G. P. Putnam's Sons   New York

For my friend
Elizabeth Garrett Jordan
a lover of Nature's World

In a quiet forest glade, where there is both sunlight and shade, stands a city of ants. Aboveground, it is a mound of twigs, leaves, and pine needles three or four feet high. All over this mound little ants run up and down, disappearing into holes or setting off on expeditions away from home. This is a nest of the wood ant, *Formica rufa*.

The ant city extends far underground, with many corridors leading to many rooms, large and small. In one of these rooms on a day in early summer little Rufa struggled out of her pupal wrappings and became an adult ant.

Rufa was a worker ant and a female, but she would never lay fertile eggs. She would work all her life for the great ant city into which she had been born.

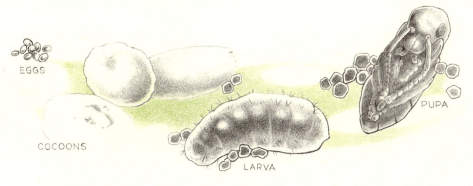

EGGS

COCOONS

PUPA

LARVA

Rufa had been alive for quite a while before this, but she had not been at all like an ant. First she was an egg, which some worker took from the queen ant as soon as it was laid and carried to another room, where it was added to a pile of eggs. When Rufa hatched from the egg, she was only a tiny worm that could hardly move. The ants did not notice her at first when they licked the eggs and turned the pile over to keep it clean. When Rufa was hungry, she reached out and ate some of the other eggs next to her! And so she grew bigger and shed her skin, and then the nurse ants saw that she was a larva, an ant baby, and no longer just an egg.

One of the nurses picked her up in its jaws and carried her to another room that was full of larvae. There she was put down on the pile, and soon an ant came and stroked her with its antenna. Little Rufa raised her head as much as she could and opened her mouth, and the ant stretched out its tongue and dropped a bit of food into her mouth. Sometimes it was chewed-up insect meat, and sometimes it was a sweet liquid. At the same time, the larva put out a sweet fluid which the nurses licked up. The sweet taste encouraged the nurse ants to keep cleaning the baby ants.

Rufa ate and grew and then had to shed her skin in order to grow more. When she had grown as much as a larva could, she shed her skin for the last time and became a pupa, wrapped in a skin without eyes or legs or a mouth. In this kind of cradle she rested for a while, and inside it she changed from a legless larva to a real ant. Now she had six legs and a long, jointed body and a head with eyes and a mouth. She had strong jaws and two long, slender antennae that waved from the top of her head. The antennae would help her to find her way about the dark streets of the ant city and to know where she was and whom she met and what they were doing.

But first she had to get out of her skin wrappings. As she struggled to free herself, she
found that another ant was helping her from
the outside. It was tearing away the old skin
and pulling her out and licking her dry. Rufa
accepted this help. She felt weak and strange
in the large room. She stood quietly while the
worker cleaned her off. She didn't even look
like the reddish-brown worker ants. She was
pale in color. She was what is called a callow.
The ants helped other callows from their pupal
shells and cleaned them off, too.

The first few days Rufa just stood around and
was fed by the nurses. Sometimes she cleaned
her antennae and her legs, scraping them off
with a little hook at the end of her two front
legs. Slowly her skin hardened, and her color

darkened, and soon she looked much like the other worker ants.

After a while, Rufa began to follow the other ants when they left the room. She followed them into the other rooms of the nest. She helped them lick the piles of eggs and turn them over to be aired. She helped them clean the larvae, and she fed the baby ants with food that other nurses had given to her. For ants have two stomachs: a crop in which they carry food back to the nest and a real stomach where they digest their own food.

Soon Rufa was doing all the things that

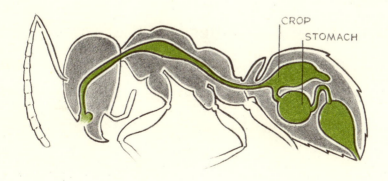

CROP

STOMACH

nurse ants do. She even helped move all the babies from their regular room to one up near the top of the nest, where they would be warmed by the sun. And when it became too hot, she helped move them back again.

Later she found her way to the special rooms where the queens were cared for. The nest had several queens, each in her own room. Each was tended by a group of worker ants, who fed and cleaned her. And each queen laid eggs all day to build up the strength of the city. Rufa helped tend the queens, and when one laid an egg, she would pick it up quickly and carry it to the pile of eggs in another room.

When Rufa was hungry, she asked another worker for food. And when she was tired, she rested. At night, when the sun went down and the nest became cold, all the ants rested and slept. The city was quiet.

Up until now, Rufa had been afraid to venture very far. If another ant made angry motions and opened its jaws at her, she ran away. But little by little she began to feel safe in the city. It was her home. And if a worker pushed or snapped at her, she snapped back and felt an urge to curl her abdomen around under her with the end pointed forward. She did not know that this was her greatest weapon, for with it she could spray formic acid at an enemy.

One day Rufa followed a corridor that led to the outdoors. She noticed that this corridor was different when she saw the light. Light was new to her and interesting. It became brighter and brighter as she followed the runway, and then she came to a door and looked out into the biggest room she had ever seen. She felt afraid. Not only was she seeing the outdoors for the first time, but she was actually seeing with her eyes for the first time as well. Inside the dark halls of the ant city she had felt her way around with her antennae.

Rufa spent several days just sitting at the door of the city and looking out. She looked at the trees and the grass and the moss. Sometimes she went away and did some work, or begged for food, or rested. But she kept coming back to the outer door. Other ants crawled over her or pushed her aside as they ran in and out. There was a guard ant that stayed by the entrance, and he pushed her aside as though she should not be there. He spent a lot of time smelling and feeling every ant that came in to be sure it belonged to the city and had a right to be there.

Then one day when things were quiet for a while and the guard ant had gone away, Rufa sat at the entrance alone. An older ant came climbing up the side of the nest. Rufa could tell it was an older worker, for it was much darker than she was and one claw on its front leg was missing.

The older ant looked around and saw that Rufa was the only one there. It came up to her and poked her with its antennae. Rufa began to beg for food, and the other ant gave her a drop of very sweet liquid. But then it poked her again. It went out of the door and turned and waved its antennae.

Rufa knew that meant "Follow me!" But to go outside the city! She moved as far as the entrance hole and stuck her head out. The other ant was halfway down the hill. Rufa took a few steps and found that it was a lot easier to go down than to go up. In fact, she almost rolled down and found herself beside the older ant more quickly than she had expected.

"Missing Claw" was pulling a twig at the
bottom of the anthill, and Rufa tried to help.
She took hold of the other end of the twig and
pulled backward as the other ant was doing.
They were pulling in opposite directions and
not getting anywhere! But gradually both ants
were able to adjust their efforts. Slowly the
twig was carried up the anthill and placed
where the older ant wanted it to go.

After that Rufa followed the ant with the missing claw. She learned to gather pine needles from around the nest and carry them up to the top. She learned to arrange them where they were most needed to keep the rain out of the city. She liked to feel the warmth of the sun and to look about at the many things outside the city. She began to feel at ease outdoors.

Each morning Rufa waited at the same entrance until Missing Claw came along. She followed the ant out the gate and down the slope. She helped the older ant in whatever task it found to do.

One day, instead of gathering pine needles and twigs for the roof, Missing Claw set off along a trail away from the city. Rufa followed. She knew that other ants had been that way because she could smell the faint odor of formic acid that all her nestmates left behind them. She knew that this was her trail, just as the city was her home.

She looked for landmarks as she followed the other ant. But Missing Claw ran so fast that Rufa could not remember everything that they passed. They went through a clump of thick grasses and around a rock. They climbed over a fallen stick and under a bunch of leaves. They came to the base of a tree. Without stopping, the older ant began to run up the trunk.

Rufa had never climbed a tree before, but she followed her leader and found that it was not very hard. The older ant found the best way to climb among the ridges of the rough bark. When they were high up in the tree, Missing Claw led Rufa to a place where a branch had been broken down. It had been blown down by the wind, and since it was still green, the sap was oozing from the break. The ants began to suck up the sap, filling their crops until they bulged with the sweet liquid.

Rufa drank and drank until she was full. She saw other ants coming up the tree, and soon she had to push her way among them to reach a good spot. When she was full, she started down the tree. Nobody had to tell her that she should take this food home to the nest.

When Rufa finally crawled through the entrance, she found crowds of workers and nurses all asking for a taste of her sweet liquid. She gave it to all who asked, even going to the nurseries to let the larvae have a drop. She was a foraging ant now, bringing food back to the city.

The next time Rufa went out to search for food she tried to keep close to Missing Claw. This worker was two or three years old and knew all the trails around the city and the best places to look for food. When the supply of sap in the tree dried up, she took Rufa foraging for insect prey.

This time they took a trail that led around the tree to an old, rotting log. Rufa watched while the other ant pushed in behind a loose piece of bark and pulled out a burrowing beetle. The older ant bit the beetle and sprayed formic acid on it, and soon the insect stopped struggling. Then the ant grabbed hold of one leg and began to drag the prey back to the city. Rufa ran up to help and took hold of another leg.

It was a long, hard haul, much more work than carrying home liquids in the crop. But Rufa kept working and helping, and as they neared the city, more ants came out and grabbed hold of the beetle. Soon they were moving faster and pushing their prey up the side of the anthill. Into a doorway it went, where dozens of other workers began to cut it up and chew it up and prepare the meat for the larvae and the queens.

Rufa left this work to the ants inside the nest. When she had rested, she went out again with her companion to look for more food. One day they found a dead butterfly to carry home. Another day it was a worm that had poked its head up in a damp spot. They needed the help of several other workers to kill the worm. But at last it was subdued and carried home and cut up to feed the thousands of ants in the city.

Rufa and Missing Claw did not kill insects all the time. One day her companion led Rufa away from the tree and the forest to a thick, bushy shrub in the glade. The ants ran up the branches and out onto the slender stems, and there Rufa saw that a length of branch was covered with little insects. They all seemed to be standing on their heads, for their beaks were thrust deep into the juicy twig. These were aphids, sucking up the sap of the bush.

Rufa rushed up and grabbed hold of an aphid
to carry it back to the nest as she had done
with the other insect prey. But just as her jaws
were about to close on an aphid, a large juicy
drop of liquid came out of its rear end and fell
into her mouth. It tasted good, like the sap
from the tree. Rufa stopped, not knowing what
to do. Was this liquid food to be carried home
in her crop? Or meat to be dragged home as
prey?

She looked and saw that Missing Claw was stepping carefully among the aphids and stroking them with her antennae. And each aphid that was stroked gave out a drop of sweet liquid which the older ant gobbled up. Rufa began to do the same and soon found it easy to "milk" the aphids of their sweet nectar.

Up and down the two ants moved among the aphids, filling their crops with the good food. Soon they were joined by other ants from the city, all busily "milking their cows." When a tiny wasp appeared and flew around the branch, the ants stood over their "cows" to protect them. They reared up at the wasp and prepared to shoot formic acid, but the wasp flew away and left the aphids alone. Rufa went home with a full crop for the city.

After that she went every day to help tend
and "milk" the aphids. Perhaps she thought it
was easier than dragging huge burdens home
to the nest. And there was always a good supply of nectar. The aphid colony grew bigger
under the care of the ants.

The city grew larger, too. The food that was being brought in by the diligent foragers fed more and more larvae. More rooms were dug to hold the eggs and offspring of the city's queens. More callows crept out of their pupal cradles and prepared to take up their work for the city.

And then one day something terrible hap-
pened. Strange bright-red ants appeared on the
trails leading to the city. At first there were
only a few, and when Rufa went out to look
at them, they ran away. But a day or two later
they came back. This time there were hundreds
of them.

Of course, there were thousands of ants in the city, and they might easily have killed the few hundred invading ants. But the city ants went into a panic. They began running about in great excitement. They seemed to know what was going to happen. But they were unable to stop it. Rufa ran about excitedly, too. She ran out of the gate, and then she ran back in again. She made threatening motions at the enemy. She curled her abdomen around to shoot formic acid. But then she changed her mind and fled into the city.

All at once a group of the red ants charged the lowest entrance gate. The guards there were bowled over. They tried to grab hold of the red ants, and here and there two ants would roll about in deadly combat. But the shock troops of the red ants got through. They paid no attention to the hundreds of city ants milling about inside. They knew what they were after. They pushed all the ants aside and dashed for the nurseries.

Rufa was knocked down by the first rush of ants. Dozens of ants walked over her. When she picked herself up, she found her companion, Missing Claw, poking her with her antenna. Obediently, she followed where the other led. They joined the stream of ants running past. Red ants and home ants were all hurrying to the brood chambers.

When they reached a room filled with pupae, they were pushed aside by the group of red ants coming out. Each one carried one of the city's sleeping children in its jaws. But instead of stopping the thieves and rescuing their babies, the city ants also grabbed up pupae and ran off with them. They wanted to save as many of their brood as possible. They wanted to move them before the red ants could get them. They ran out the gates and down the anthill. There the red ants were waiting in a circle around the

city. Each worker that came down with a pupa or a larva had its burden grabbed away by the waiting ants, who promptly ran off home with it to their city.

Rufa and her companion each picked up a pupa and ran out of the room. They ran as fast as they could, and they tried to avoid the invading red ants. Of course, they could not see which ant was red in the darkness of the nest. But they could smell. Each nest and the ants in it have a special smell. Rufa's antennae told her when an enemy was near, and she quickly escaped up a side street.

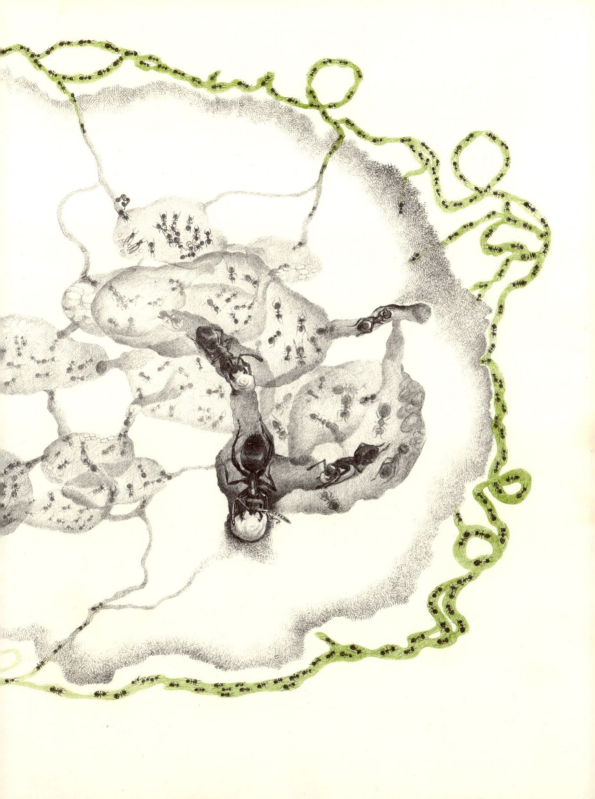

They left the city by one of the upper gates.
Outside they stopped a minute to rest. They
could hear the turmoil still going on inside the
city. They could see their nestmates pouring
out of the lower entrances, each carrying a pupa
or a larva. They watched as the waiting red ants
pounced upon them and seized their precious
burdens. Perhaps there were cries and wails too
high for human ears to hear.

Suddenly, a group of the red ants saw the two brown ants on the higher level. They began to run up the anthill. Rufa and the older worker turned to flee. But they were hindered by the loads they carried. The red ants had no burdens and held nothing in their jaws. They caught up with Missing Claw and piled on top of her, biting and clawing and trying to shoot formic acid.

Rufa had a moment for escape. She ran as fast as she could to the top of the city and hid in the newly laid pine thatch. When she looked out, she saw Missing Claw rolling slowly down the anthill with three red ants biting at her and holding to her legs. She wanted to go to help the older ant, but she dared not put down the pupa that she carried. She could do nothing as long as she held this burden in her jaws, and instinct told her that the pupa was vital to the life of the city.

The battle had begun at noon, and it went on until late in the day. When the last red ant had disappeared with its stolen treasure (destined to live as slaves in the red ants' nest), Rufa carried her pupa back into the city.

Inside everything was confusion. Galleries and rooms were broken and dirty. Eggs and larvae and pupae were strewn about. The queens were so disturbed that they had stopped laying. And the workers were still running about in wild excitement, looking for the red ants that were no longer there.

Rufa took her burden to the proper room and began to put things in order. She helped to bring back any of the brood that the red ants had dropped and to repair the broken city streets. She helped feed the hungry brood and went to clean and stroke the queens until they were once more calm and at peace.

As she ran about the city streets and helped with these tasks, Rufa now and then noticed a dark form in a corner. These were the dead ants, killed in the fighting. When more important work had been done, the city ants took notice of them. The corpses were taken and thrown on the city dump, where all the dirt and refuse of the nest was cast. And there a clean-up gang threw the body of Missing Claw, which they picked up at the foot of the anthill. Rufa never saw her again.

After the battle with the red slave-making
ants, Rufa worked harder than ever. The whole
city was busy, repairing the damage to the
nest, feeding and cleaning the queens so that
they would lay more eggs, and caring for the
growing brood.

In a few weeks the rooms were again filled with eggs, and larvae and pupae and new ants were coming out of their cradles. Rufa sensed a different air about the nest. There was a feeling of excitement everywhere. When she went into a room with food for the callow ants, she saw that many of them had wings. They were bigger than the worker ants, with larger eyes. They stood quietly with their wings folded along their backs and ate the food that she brought.

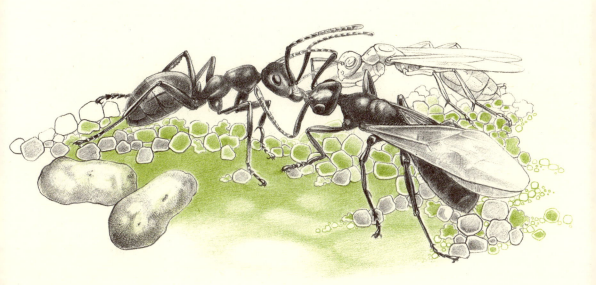

After a few days, when they were stronger, the winged ants began to move about the city. They were so big that they filled the city streets. These were the males and females that would build new ant cities. They began to chase each other around the nest. They wanted to get out and try their wings. They wanted to find mates. But the workers would not let the winged ants out until the weather was just right. They closed all the city gates with guards and tried to keep the males and females apart inside the nest.

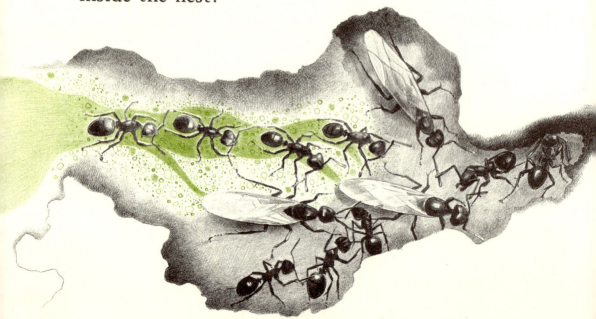

The excitement in the city rose almost to the
boiling point. Thousands of ants were milling
about inside. Rufa brought her loads of food
to the gates of the city and there gave it to
the guards and the workers. Then she rushed
off to find more and hurried back for a look
at the winged ants.

At last the right day came. It was cloudy
but warm and without rain. In the afternoon
the guards and the workers opened the city
gates. They had to make the doors larger so
that these ants would not scrape their wings.
Then a huge swarm rushed out of the city. The
air was thick with flying ants.

The same swarming was going on in other
nests in the area. The swarms of winged males
and females from different cities met and mixed
in the air. Around and around swirled the
young ants, the males trying to find the females
in the mad dance. Many of them only found
each other when they fell to the ground.

All kinds of birds and animals knew about the ants' swarming. They snapped up the ants as fast as they came out of the holes. But some got away.

Sometimes a fertile queen found her way back into the nest. There she began to lay eggs and was cared for by the workers. Sometimes a young queen would go off with a group of workers from her old nest. They would build a new nest nearby. Then the ants would run back and forth between the two nests. The new nest was like a suburb of the ant city.

Little Rufa went back into the city. She was tired and needed to rest. The excitement of the swarming was over. She joined a group of ants that was cleaning up the debris left by the milling swarm. But she had little energy left for work. When she had taken out one load, she came back in and found a niche in a corner. She hid there and rested.

She was almost asleep when an ant came up and stroked her with its antenna. It was begging for food, and Rufa gave it a drop of liquid from her crop. She had very little left. She reached out to touch the ant with her antennae and felt that it was a different kind of ant. It did not have the same kind of hard, smooth skin. It wasn't an ant at all—it was a beetle!

Rufa had seen these beetles before. There were quite a few of them living in the nest. In fact, the city housed a variety of visitors of all kinds who found the ants' city a safe and comfortable place to live. Mostly the ants paid little attention to them. Now and then one would be chased out or killed before it could get away.

This beetle had hairs on its body, and Rufa began to lick the hairs. A most delightful taste came into her mouth. It was something like the juices of the aphids, only better. Rufa licked over all the beetle's hairs and gave it another drop to eat, and then she settled down in her niche and went to sleep. Rufa missed the older worker ant with the missing claw. The beetle made her feel safe and cozy. She could rest contented.

The end of the year was coming for the ants. The cold time that brought the long sleep. Ants do not store food as the bees do. They must pass the winter in sleep. A sleep that we call hibernation.

Rufa spent less and less time outdoors. She went a little way on the trails each day, but then she returned to the city. It was getting colder, even when the sun shone. Insects cannot move well in the cold. They slow down and they die. Rufa found that the aphids were all gone from the tree pastures. Some had been carried into the city by the ants. They were placed upon roots far underground, where they could survive the winter.

One day Rufa did not go outdoors at all. She stayed in the city with the other ants. She rested and licked the hairs of the beetle, but she had very little food to give it in return.

Even the nest was growing cold now. The well-thatched roof of the dome could no longer keep out the winter wind. Rufa followed the other ants down into the lower parts of the city. Deep in the earth they crowded together. They formed closely packed swarms with the queens at the centers. They slept, but they moved in their sleep. They moved around and around, and the ants on the outside burrowed in, and ones inside moved out. In this way all of them were warmed part of the time. And the queens, who made life for the city, were warm and protected all winter.

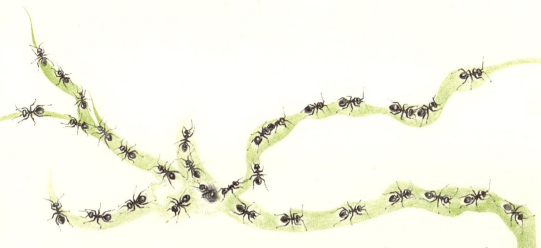

After the winter the spring would come, and little Rufa would wake up and begin to work again. The city would come to life. There would be hustling and bustling and the ants running in all directions. For the city must be fed. The city must be repaired. And new defenses must be made against its enemies.

The Author

Alice L. Hopf is equally at home writing science fiction (under her maiden name, A. M. Lightner) and writing about nature. She is a member of the Lepidopterists Society, the New York Entomological Society, and the Audubon Society. She has written several other nature and animal books for Putnam's, including *Butterfly and Moth, Carab the Trap-Door Spider, Biography of an Octopus, Biography of a Rhino,* and *Wild Cousins of the Dog.*

The Artist

Jean Zallinger was only thirteen when she started earning her own money to attend classes at the Museum School in Boston. Later she went to the Massachusetts School of Art and on to win a fellowship to the Yale School of Fine Arts. There she met her husband, Rudolph, the well-known naturalist painter who won the Pulitzer Art Prize for his mural of dinosaurs in the Peabody Museum of Natural History at Yale. Both Zallingers now teach at the Paier Art School in Connecticut.